# Susan B. Anthony

History Maker Bios

**Stephanie Sammartino McPherson**

⫧ LERNER PUBLICATIONS COMPANY • MINNEAPOLIS

*For my mother, Marion Sammartino, who has always stood up for her beliefs and who raised her daughters to believe they could do anything. And to the memory of my friend Johanna Verhaagen, who told the registrar of voters almost eighty years ago, "One of these fine days, a woman is going to be president."*

*Thanks to Richard McPherson and Angelo Sammartino for their careful reading of this manuscript and to my editor, Sara Hoffmann, for her insightful comments and suggestions.*

Illustrations by Tim Parlin

Text copyright © 2006 by Stephanie Sammartino McPherson
Illustrations copyright © 2006 by Lerner Publications Company

Lerner Publications Company
A division of Lerner Publishing Group
241 First Avenue North
Minneapolis, MN 55401 U.S.A.

Website address: www.lernerbooks.com

Library of Congress Cataloging-in-Publication Data

McPherson, Stephanie Sammartino.
    Susan B. Anthony / Stephanie McPherson.
        p.    cm. — (History maker bios)
    Includes bibliographical references and index.
    ISBN-13: 978-0-8225-5938-2 (lib. bdg. : alk. paper)
    ISBN-10: 0-8225-5938-2 (lib. bdg. : alk. paper)
        1. Anthony, Susan B. (Susan Brownell), 1820–1906—Juvenile literature.
    2. Feminists—United States—Biography—Juvenile literature. 3. Suffragists—
    United States—Biography—Juvenile literature. 4. Women's rights—United
    States—History—Juvenile literature. I. Title. II. Series.
    HQ1413.A55M389 2006
    305.42092—dc22                                                    2005033272

Manufactured in the United States of America
1  2  3  4  5  6  –  JR  –  11  10  09  08  07  06

# TABLE OF CONTENTS

# INTRODUCTION

**S**usan B. Anthony believed in freedom. She wanted men and women to have the same rights. In Susan's lifetime, only men could vote. Susan thought women should be allowed to vote too.

Susan fought hard for woman's rights. She also tried to help African Americans. Until 1865, slavery was legal in many parts of the United States. Susan thought slavery was wrong. She spoke out against it.

Susan did not live to see women win the right to vote. But she never lost faith in the future. "Failure is impossible," she declared.

This is her story.

# 1GROWING UP QUAKER

**S**usan Brownell Anthony was born on February 15, 1820, near Adams, Massachusetts. Few people at that time thought girls could learn as much as boys. But Susan was very smart. She learned to read before she was four years old.

Susan's father, Daniel, was proud of her. Daniel was a Quaker. This religious group believed that education was important for girls as well as boys.

Quakers also believed in living simply. They wore plain, gray clothes. They called one another thee and thou. The Anthony children had few toys. Susan's father wanted his children to lead quiet lives. Susan loved to take long walks with her sisters. She picked wildflowers and watched animals.

*Susan was born in this house near Adams, Massachusetts.*

A girl peels vegetables. In the early 1800s, even very young girls helped with meals.

When Susan was six, her family moved to Battenville, New York. In Battenville, Daniel ran a large cotton mill. Soon he became one of the richest people in town. But Susan still had to do chores. Susan sewed. She cooked. She lugged buckets of water to the house. About one dozen young women who worked at the mill lived in the Anthony home. Susan's mother welcomed them. But their presence meant lots of cooking and lots of dishes to wash.

One day, Susan got a chance to see what a mill girl's life was really like. One of her father's workers got sick. Susan took her place at the loom. She wove thread into cloth on this large wooden machine. Susan's father paid her three dollars for two weeks at the loom. He paid the men more money for their work. Susan decided to buy her mother a gift with the money. She chose six blue coffee cups and saucers.

*Looms weave thread into long pieces of cloth.*

Susan could have bought more cups if she made as much money as the men. But something bothered her more. When she was about twelve years old, one of the bosses at her father's mill left. Susan knew Sally Ann Hyatt was a good weaver. Susan thought Sally should become the new boss.

Daniel Anthony said no. A woman could not be a boss, he explained. Susan didn't understand. If a woman was a good worker, why couldn't she have a better job?

Many women worked at Daniel's cotton mill. But he didn't think a woman could be a boss. This bothered Susan.

*Susan's parents, Daniel and Lucy Read Anthony, married in 1817.*

In 1833, the Anthonys moved. Their new home was big. There was plenty of space for Susan, her older sister, and five younger brothers and sisters.

Susan loved her family deeply. When her father sent her to boarding school in Pennsylvania, she missed them. But Susan wasn't away long. Daniel's business failed. He didn't have enough money to keep Susan in school. He could no longer afford their home. The family moved to a house that had once been a tavern. The house was in Hardscrabble, New York. Susan thought the town was every bit as bad as its name sounded.

## Few Rights for Women

Women had few rights in the early 1800s. When a woman married, everything she owned became the property of her husband. Susan's mother had nothing to call her own. All her goods had to be sold to pay her husband's debts. According to the law, her husband also had the final say on everything concerning their children. He could even take them away if he wished.

When she was younger, Susan had taken summer teaching jobs. Her father thought teaching would help Susan and her older sister, Guelma, become responsible young women. In 1839, Susan began teaching again to help her family. She had no other choice.

# 2 INDEPENDENT YOUNG WOMAN

**S**usan's grandparents wanted to give some money to her mother, Lucy. They didn't want the money to be used to pay Daniel's debts. So they left the money to Lucy's uncle. Since he was a man, he could choose what to do with the money. He could use it to help the Anthonys. In 1845, he bought a farm near Rochester, New York, for Susan's parents.

Soon there was more good news. Susan became the head of the girls' section at a school in Canajoharie, New York. Susan was strict. But she was a popular teacher. She played games and shared jokes with her students. She took them on field trips.

Susan was living with people who were not Quakers. She began to copy their ways. Instead of "thee," she said "you." She wore bright colors instead of gray dresses.

Susan started teaching school in 1839.

*Susan believed she should marry only if she met the right man.*

Young men noticed Susan. She was friendly and had a good sense of humor. Several men asked her to marry them. Susan enjoyed dating, but she did not fall in love with anyone. Most women in the 1800s felt they had to be married. But not Susan. If the right man came along, that would be fine. If not, Susan would take care of herself.

Two workers (LEFT) and family members ask a man to sign a statement. It is a promise to stop drinking liquor.

Susan was busy, but she paid close attention to current events. She heard a lot about the temperance movement. It was about outlawing liquor. Some men spent all their money on alcoholic drinks. They didn't leave anything to buy food or clothing for their children. Susan wanted to change this. She joined a temperance group in 1849.

At the age of twenty-nine, Susan was tired of teaching. She earned only $2.50 a week. Men doing the same job received $10 a week. Susan wanted to do something different with her life. A man named James Marshall had discovered gold in California. Other men from across the country headed west to make their fortunes. Most people did not think women could handle such an adventure. But the gold rush of 1849 excited Susan. "Oh, if I were [only] a man so that I could go!" she wrote.

*Susan wanted to join the California gold rush of 1849.*

Susan's father knew she needed a change. He said she could run the farm in Rochester. Susan directed the planting and the harvesting. She took charge of selling the crops.

On the farm, Susan began to think more about slavery. Slavery was still legal in the United States. White slave owners forced African Americans to work without pay.

*On farms in the South, slaves picked cotton from dawn to dusk. It was hard work. But the slaves received no money.*

A former slave, Frederick Douglass (SEATED, FRONT RIGHT), attended antislavery meetings on the Anthonys' farm.

Susan's father had become involved in the abolitionist movement. Abolitionists wanted to abolish, or end, slavery. They tried to convince others that all men, women, and children should be free. Sometimes twenty guests would gather at the Anthony house. They discussed slavery and ate dinner. Susan prepared the meals. She wanted the food to be perfect. But she didn't want to miss a word of the conversation. She raced back and forth between the kitchen and the parlor.

*People caught helping slaves escape from their owners could be put in jail.*

Susan and her family also worked with the Underground Railroad. This secret group helped runaway slaves escape to freedom in the North. It had nothing to do with trains. It was called a railroad because of the many roads slaves traveled on while escaping.

In 1851, an important abolitionist meeting was held in Seneca Falls, New York. Susan went to hear the speeches with her new friend, Amelia Bloomer. In Seneca Falls, Susan met Amelia's friend Elizabeth Cady Stanton.

Susan and Elizabeth liked each other right away. Susan had already heard of Elizabeth. She knew they shared many ideas. Later that summer, Susan returned to Seneca Falls for another meeting. Elizabeth asked Susan to stay at her home. The two became close friends.

## WOMEN WANT TO BE HEARD

Elizabeth Cady Stanton was against slavery. In 1840, she went to a World Anti-Slavery Convention in Great Britain. There she met Lucretia Mott, a Quaker minister. Elizabeth and Lucretia wanted to speak at the convention. But the leaders would not let them. Women were not allowed to speak in public. Elizabeth and Lucretia promised each other that one day they would change things. Eight years later, they held the United States' first woman's rights convention in Seneca Falls, New York.

Susan continued her temperance work. She spent many weeks going from door to door with petitions. She asked people to sign these statements. The petitions asked lawmakers to stop the sale of liquor. If Susan got enough signatures, the lawmakers might listen.

In January 1852, Susan went to a meeting of the Sons of Temperance. People came from all around the state. Susan tried to join the discussion. But the leader of the group would not let her. He said that women "were not invited to speak . . . but to listen and learn." Susan was stunned. Angrily, she walked out of the meeting.

# 3 HER OWN STRONG VOICE

**S**usan found something to do with her anger. She started a temperance society just for women. To start things off right, she asked Elizabeth Stanton to speak to the group. Susan knew Elizabeth was a fine speaker. Susan was better at organizing events than at making speeches. Together Susan and Elizabeth made a powerful team. The new group elected Elizabeth president and Susan secretary.

In September 1852, Susan went to Syracuse, New York, for her first woman's rights convention. Susan heard many good speeches. But some of the other women did not speak loudly enough to be heard. They were afraid they wouldn't seem ladylike if they spoke up. Susan had no time for such silliness. "We do not stand up here to be seen, but to be heard," she declared in her own strong voice.

## A BRIDE'S PROTEST

Lucy Stone was another famous woman's rights leader. Like her friend Susan, she did not agree with marriage laws that took away women's freedom. When Lucy married Henry Blackwell, the couple wrote a protest against these laws into the wedding ceremony. Lucy was the first American woman to keep her own last name after marriage. Later women to do this became known as Lucy Stoners.

*Amelia Bloomer gave speeches. She also published the Lily from 1849 to 1854. It was a temperance newspaper for women. It also published many woman's rights articles.*

Susan spent the spring of 1853 traveling through New York. She gave temperance lectures with her friend Amelia Bloomer. Wherever the women went, they set up new temperance groups.

By that time, Susan had traded in her skirts for a new style called bloomers. Susan liked the short skirt worn over baggy pants. But there was a price to pay for wearing bloomers. Many people thought the fashion was shocking. Some men made rude remarks when they saw women wearing bloomers. Susan thought people paid more attention to her bloomers than to her speeches. After about one year, she stopped wearing them.

Amelia Bloomer did not invent bloomers (LEFT). But she put an ad for them in her newspaper. The ad helped make the baggy pants popular. They became known as bloomers.

*Elizabeth Cady Stanton appears in this photograph with her son Henry, who was born in 1844.*

Bloomers weren't Susan's only problem. Susan and Elizabeth held the second meeting of their temperance group in 1853. The members voted to let men join. They also wanted to change their group's focus. They didn't want to work for woman's rights anymore. They decided Elizabeth could no longer be president. Once again, Susan was angry. She quit the group. But Elizabeth wasn't upset. She said that woman's rights were more important than temperance.

*Like Elizabeth Cady Stanton (LEFT), Susan gave many lectures through the years. Her earnings helped to pay for her woman's rights work.*

Susan agreed with her friend. She went on a speaking tour of New York State to raise money for woman's rights conventions. Just one year earlier, she had set up women's temperance groups in the same area. To her disappointment, most of these groups had disappeared. The women didn't have enough money to keep the groups going. Their husbands had not helped them. Women needed to have their own money, Susan realized.

Susan began planning ways to help women get control of their money. She wanted married women to be able to own property. She organized sixty women to go from door-to-door throughout New York State. They would collect signatures on petitions to take to the state capital in Albany.

Susan set out with petitions too. She also asked people to sign a statement supporting suffrage for women. *Suffrage* means "the right to vote." Many people were amazed at the idea of women voting. But Susan was determined. She did not give up when the lawmakers ignored her petitions.

*Women present a petition to state lawmakers in Albany, New York.*

# 4 SUSAN ON THE ROAD

Susan took to the road to gather even more signatures. She began her new tour on Christmas Day 1854. Snow often blocked the roads. But Susan kept a busy schedule.

People still thought it was shocking for a woman to speak in public. Many came to Susan's talks just to stare. Susan got attention. But the lawmakers didn't take her demands seriously.

Year after year, Susan flooded the state government with petitions. In 1856, she also became part of the American Anti-Slavery Society. This group sent out speakers to convince people that slavery was wrong. Susan worked hard for the society. She never seemed to run out of energy.

Susan counted on her friend Elizabeth to help her. She was happy to share Elizabeth's household chores. Susan also enjoyed playing with and taking care of Elizabeth's children. They called her Aunt Susan.

*This is part of an antislavery speech Susan wrote in 1859. She calls slavery in the United States a "startling fact."*

We are assembled here, this evening, for the purpose of discussing the question of american Slavery: — — The startling fact that there are in these United States, under the sanction of this professedly Christian, Republican Government, nearly Four millions of human beings now clanking the chains of Slavery: —

The two friends helped each other prepare speeches. "I am the better writer, she the better critic," Elizabeth wrote. "Our speeches may be considered the united product of two brains."

In 1860, lawmakers passed the Married Women's Property Act. Married women in New York would have a right to control the money they earned. They could make decisions for their children. Later, women would lose some of these rights. But for a time, they had won a huge victory.

*The U.S. Mint in Philadelphia, Pennsylvania, hired women in the 1850s. They measured coins. At this time, most marrried women had no right to keep the money they earned.*

Susan was eager to win more rights for women. Then the Civil War (1861–1865) began. The North fought the South over slavery. People were too worried about the war to think about woman's rights.

## TRUE LOYALTY

During the Civil War, Susan and Elizabeth started the Women's National Loyal League. Members of this group wanted freedom for slaves. President Abraham Lincoln had freed some slaves. But the Loyal League wanted *all* slaves to be free. At the group's first meeting, Lucy Stone explained that everyone has rights. If the women ignored the rights of a single person, they would "fail in [their] loyalty to the country." In 1865, the Thirteenth Amendment said that all slavery must end.

This is a handwritten copy of the Fourteenth (XIV) Amendment of the U.S. Constitution.

One morning, after the war ended, Susan picked up a newspaper. The paper said that Congress was thinking about changing the U.S. Constitution. The change, called the Fourteenth Amendment, would make the freed slaves citizens. Black males would have the same rights as white males.

Susan stared at the paper. What was the word *male* doing in the Fourteenth Amendment? This would make it harder for women to get the right to vote. Susan knew it was time to get people thinking about woman's rights again.

Susan tried to convince lawmakers to give suffrage to women in Kansas. The law failed. But Susan had more plans. She started a newspaper called the *Revolution*. The paper's motto was "Men, their rights and nothing more; women, their rights and nothing less." The first issue came out on January 1, 1868.

Susan lost the battle to include women in the Fourteenth Amendment. Soon a Fifteenth Amendment came up for discussion. Susan did not like this amendment any better. It said that people could vote regardless of race. But it said nothing about women.

*Susan published her newspaper for two years.*

# The Revolution.

PRINCIPLE, NOT POLICY: JUSTICE, NOT FAVORS.—MEN, THEIR RIGHTS AND NOTHING MORE; WOMEN, THEIR RIGHTS AND NOTHING LESS.

VOL. I.—NO. 16.   NEW YORK, THURSDAY, APRIL 23, 1868.   $2 A YEAR.
SINGLE COPY 10 CENTS.

## The Revolution.

ELIZABETH CADY STANTON,
PARKER PILLSBURY,  } Editors.
SUSAN B. ANTHONY, Proprietor.

OFFICE 37 PARK ROW (ROOM 17).

THEODORE DREAMING, WITH FLAG AT HALF MAST.

LAST week's *Independent*, in a long column, throws Mr. Chase overboard, clears the track for Grant, and gets itself ready to wheel into

stitute another name, it might be the name of Charles Sumner, or Schuyler Colfax, or Ben Wade, or Gen. Butler. But, of course, the Chicago Convention will go pell mell for Gen. Grant. Nevertheless, we shall go on dreaming our day-dream of the happy day when only a great statesman shall be eligible to preside over the Great Republic.

This happy day is to be ushered in by teaching the people how to choose their leaders; that the best interests of the nation do not depend on the success of any party, but on the virtue and education of the people. Why go "pell-mell" for Grant when all admit that he is unfit for the position? It is not too late, if true men and women will do their duty, to make an honest man like Ben Wade President.

more easily led *en masse* than the more cultivated Mrs. Howards.

People who see two right sides to a question generally fail to see either side clearly. All questions of importance, such as relate to human rights, are so perfectly clear to those who see them at all, that both the right and the wrong side stand out in bold relief. It seems to us that neither Gail Hamilton nor her reviewer comprehends the deep significance of this question of universal suffrage. In reading this book we were struck with its weakness the moment the author lost sight of Todd and undertook to reason. Like the cat with a mouse, she was wide awake and intensely active until her victim was no more; then came a reaction that

A meeting of a woman suffrage association

Susan helped start a woman suffrage group. The group fought against the Fifteenth Amendment because it did not include women. Some women supported the amendment because it gave black men the vote. They started their own group.

By then, Susan was famous. Her courage made her a hero to many people. Others disliked her. Since Susan talked so much about woman's rights, they figured she must be against men. Such people did not really know Susan. She had a warm personality. She enjoyed friendships with both men and women.

Susan worked hard on her newspaper. But printing costs were expensive. The *Revolution* was losing money. Finally, she had to sell the paper. She had lots of bills to pay. Susan raised money by giving lectures. It took many years, but she paid every penny of the money she owed.

*In one year, Susan traveled 13,000 miles to give 171 lectures.*

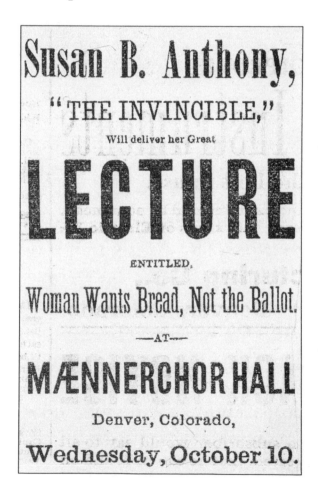

Susan B. Anthony,
"THE INVINCIBLE,"
Will deliver her Great
LECTURE
ENTITLED,
Woman Wants Bread, Not the Ballot.
—AT—
MÆNNERCHOR HALL
Denver, Colorado,
Wednesday, October 10.

# 5 ONLY ONE WISH

Some people thought that women already had the right to vote. The Fourteenth Amendment said that everyone born in the United States was a citizen. That meant that women were citizens. And citizens had the right to vote.

Did that mean that women could vote? Fifty-two-year-old Susan was determined to find out. She decided to vote for president in 1872. Two weeks after she voted for Ulysses S. Grant, a marshal came to arrest her.

The courtroom was full when Susan came to trial on June 17, 1873. After the lawyers spoke, the judge responded. He said the state government of New York had decided that only men could vote. He said that Susan knew this. Then he told the jury to find her guilty. He asked Susan if there was any reason why she should not be sentenced.

Susan was arrested at her home in Rochester, New York.

## THE WOMAN WHO DARED.

Close of the Trial of Susan B. Anthony.

### OPINION AND DECISION OF JUDGE HUNT.

The Fourteenth Amendment Gives No Right to a Woman to Vote.

MISS ANTHONY'S ACT A VIOLATION OF LAW.

Exhaustive Opinion on the Force and Scope of the Amendments.

A VERDICT OF GUILTY.

The Champion of Woman's Rights Awaiting Sentence and Martyrdom.

Susan had so many reasons that she could not stop speaking. The judge tried to silence her. But Susan kept talking. Finally, the judge fined her $100. "I shall never pay a dollar of your unjust penalty," replied Susan. She never did.

Nothing could stop Susan. She was as comfortable with presidents as she was with ordinary folks. One time, while she was walking in Washington, D.C., she met President Grant. Politely the president asked what he could do for her. "I have only one wish, Mr. President," replied Susan, "and that is to see women vote."

*Ulysses S. Grant was the U.S. president from 1869 to 1877.*

*Susan and Elizabeth's history book was six volumes long. The women worked together on the first four volumes.*

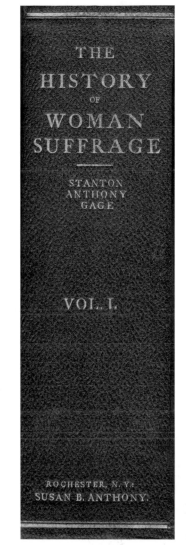

THE
HISTORY
OF
WOMAN
SUFFRAGE

STANTON
ANTHONY
GAGE

VOL. I.

ROCHESTER, N. Y.:
SUSAN B. ANTHONY.

Susan took this message on speaking tours across the country. She also worked with Elizabeth Cady Stanton on a book called *The History of Woman Suffrage*. But Susan didn't enjoy the project. She said she would "rather make history than write it."

When Susan was seventy-five, she became president of the National American Woman Suffrage Association. "I find the older I get, the greater power I have to help the world," she told reporter Nellie Bly. "I am like a snowball—the further I am rolled, the more I gain." Susan meant that the harder she worked, the better she got.

*Susan (AT RIGHT) and Elizabeth were friends for more than fifty years.*

Susan kept rolling through 1896 when she spoke for voting rights in California. But the law that would have given women the vote did not pass. Susan had better luck closer to home. Most colleges then did not allow women to attend. Susan helped convince the University of Rochester to accept women students.

In 1902, Elizabeth Cady Stanton died. Susan had lost her best friend. But she continued to travel. She made her last speech on her eighty-sixth birthday in Washington, D.C. After returning home, she became ill with pneumonia. She died on March 13, 1906.

## State by State

In 1868, an amendment that would give the vote to women first came before Congress. It failed. It continued to fail for many years. But women knew of another way to get the vote. Individual states could pass their own laws. In 1869, the Wyoming territory granted woman suffrage. By 1900, Utah, Idaho, and Colorado had also given women the right to vote. By the time the Susan B. Anthony Amendment passed in 1920, fifteen states and two territories allowed women to vote in all elections.

Thousands of women remembered Susan's brave words. They continued to fight for woman's rights. In 1920, the Nineteenth Amendment—also called the Susan B. Anthony Amendment—gave women the right to vote. It is the only memorial Susan would have wanted.

# TIMELINE

SUSAN B. ANTHONY WAS BORN NEAR ADAMS, MASSACHUSETTS, ON FEBRUARY 15, 1820.

## *In the year . . .*

1839   Susan took a teaching job to help her family.   Age 19

1846   she became the head of the girls' section at a school in Canajoharie, New York.

1851   she met Elizabeth Cady Stanton.

1852   Susan started a women's temperance group in New York.

1853   she began collecting signatures on petitions calling for property rights for women.

1856   she began working for the American Anti-Slavery Society.   Age 36

1860   the Married Women's Property Act became law in New York.

1861   the Civil War began.

1865   the Civil War ended.
the Thirteenth Amendment outlawed slavery.

1868   the first issue of the *Revolution* appeared on January 1.
the Fourteenth Amendment made former slaves citizens.

1870   the Fifteenth Amendment gave African American men the right to vote.

1872   Susan voted in the presidential election.   Age 52

1873   she was brought to trial for voting.

1895   she became president of the National American Woman Suffrage Association.   Age 75

1906   she died on March 13.   Age 86

1920   the Nineteenth Amendment gave women the right to vote.

# CELEBRATING A CENTURY

In 1876, the United States celebrated its one hundredth birthday. But Susan didn't think that women had as much to celebrate as men did. She wanted the women of the United States to present a declaration of their rights during a ceremony on the Fourth of July. She felt this was a good way to show that women were still fighting for their rights.

The special event took place at Independence Hall in Philadelphia, Pennsylvania. Susan and her companions waited for the Declaration of Independence to be read. Then they hurried forward to present their own declaration. People stood on chairs to grab the copies that the women passed out afterward.

Susan went outside and stood by the Liberty Bell. "We ask . . . no special favors," she read. "We ask justice, we ask equality, we ask that all the civil and political rights that belong to citizens of the United States be guaranteed to us and our daughters forever."

*Many U.S. citizens celebrated their nation's one hundredth birthday in Philadelphia on July 4, 1876. This man read the Declaration of Independence. Then Susan gave her speech.*

# Further Reading

NONFICTION

**Hossell, Karen Price. *The Nineteenth Amendment: Women Get the Vote*. Chicago: Heinemann Library, 2003.** This book includes sections on the first woman's rights convention, women in World War I, the Nineteenth Amendment, and women in government.

**Moore, Kay. *If You Lived at the Time of the Civil War.* New York: Scholastic, 1994.** This book explains what life was like in the North and in the South during the Civil War.

FICTION

**McCully, Emily Arnold. *The Ballot Box Battle*. New York: Dragonfly Books, 1998.** In this picture book, Cordelia learns a valuable lesson from her neighbor Elizabeth Cady Stanton.

**White, Linda Arms. *I Could Do That!: Esther Morris Gets Women the Vote*. New York: Farrar, Straus, and Giroux, 2005.** This title tells the story of Esther Morris, who won the vote for women in Wyoming.

# Websites

**National Women's Hall of Fame**
http://www.greatwomen.org This website allows you to look up the accomplishments of inspiring American women.

**Susan B. Anthony House**
http://www.susanbanthonyhouse.org This website includes a biography, timeline, and virtual tour of Susan B. Anthony's house in Rochester, New York.

# SELECT BIBLIOGRAPHY

Barry, Kathleen. *Susan B. Anthony: A Biography of a Singular Feminist*. New York: New York University Press, 1988.

Buhle, Mari Jo, and Paul Buhle, eds. *The Concise History of Woman Suffrage: Selections from the Classic Work of Stanton, Anthony, Gage, and Harper*. Urbana: University of Illinois Press, 1978.

Gurko, Miriam. *The Ladies of Seneca Falls: The Birth of the Woman's Rights Movement*. New York: Schocken Books, 1974.

Harper, Ida Husted. *The Life and Work of Susan B. Anthony*. 3 vols. Indianapolis: Bowen-Merrill Co., 1899–1908.

Sherr, Lynn. *Failure Is Impossible: Susan B. Anthony in Her Own Words*. New York: Random House/Times Books, 1995.

Ward, Geoffrey C., and Ken Burns. *Not for Ourselves Alone: The Story of Elizabeth Cady Stanton and Susan B. Anthony*. New York: Alfred A. Knopf, 1999.

# INDEX

## Acknowledgments

**For photographs and artwork:** © Brown Brothers, pp. 4, 15, 29; Library of Congress, pp. 7 (LC-USZ62-111870), 16 (LC-USZ62-90146), 17 (LC-USZ62-740), 26 (LC-USZC2-1978), 31 (LC-DIG-ppmsca-02934), 40 (LC-USZ62-13018), 42 (LC-USZ61-791), 45 (LC-USZ62-112732); © North Wind Picture Archives, pp. 8, 9, 10; © Archive Photos/Getty Images, p. 14; From the Collection of the Madison County Historical Society, Oneida, New York, p. 19; C.T. Webber, *The Underground Railway*, Cincinnati Art Museum, p. 20; Dictionary of American Portraits, p. 25; Coline Jenkins/Elizabeth Cady Stanton Trust, pp. 27, 35, 36, 41; © Bettmann/CORBIS, p. 28; © CORBIS, p. 32; © Hulton Archive/Getty Images, p. 34; Library of Congress, Rare Books Division, Susan B. Anthony Scrapbooks, pp. 37 (vol. 8, p. 147), 39 (vol. 6 (4b), p. 126). Front Cover: © CORBIS. Back Cover: Coline Jenkins/Elizabeth Cady Stanton Trust.
**For quoted material:** pp. 5, 40, and 41, Lynn Sherr, *Failure Is Impossible: Susan B. Anthony in Her Own Words* (New York: Random House/Times Books, 1995); pp. 17 and 32, Miriam Gurko, *The Ladies of Seneca Falls: The Birth of the Woman's Rights Movement* (New York: Schocken Books, 1974); pp. 22 and 24, Geoffrey C. Ward and Ken Burns, *Not for Ourselves Alone: The Story of Elizabeth Cady Stanton and Susan B. Anthony* (New York: Alfred A. Knopf, 1999); p. 34, Kathleen Barry, *Susan B. Anthony: A Biography of a Singular Feminist* (New York: New York University Press, 1988); pp. 33 and 45, Mari Jo Buhle and Paul Buhle, eds., *The Concise History of Woman Suffrage: Selections from the Classic Work of Stanton, Anthony, Gage, and Harper* (Urbana: University of Illinois Press, 1978).